Beyond
the Stigma
of Abuse

Beyond the Stigma of Abuse

By Linda Wasil

Big Country Publishing, LLC

Beyond the Stigma of Abuse
Copyright© 2012 by Linda Wasil
Library of Congress Control Number: 2001012345
ISBN: 978-1-938487-02-6
eBook ISBN: 978-1-93848707-1

Cover design by Kyle Petrove
Cover photography © Rikka Zimmerman
First Printing 2012

Published by
Big Country Publishing, LLC
7691 Shaffer Parkway, Suite C
Littleton, CO 80127
USA
www.bigcountrypublishing.com

Printed in USA, UK, Australia

Acknowledgments

I'd like to thank you, the reader, for choosing my book. How did I get so lucky? Thank you so much for having the courage and strength to trust your knowing and to choose something different. Thank you for knowing that something else IS possible. You just have to choose it.

I'm grateful for so many phenomenal people in my life that have contributed to this book. You know who you are! First off, I'd like to thank Gary Douglas, the founder of Access Consciousness™, and his business partner, Dr. Dain Heer. I'm so grateful that they empowered me to know what was true for me, and that I wasn't as f$%!# up as I thought I was. They also gave me the tools to create a life beyond what I could imagine. What else is possible?

I'd also like to thank Simone Milasas for her encouragement and support of this project along with Blossom, Fiona, Heather, Suzy, and the rest of the Access team. You guys rock!

I'd also like to thank the amazing animal beings in my life. My playful puppy, Coco, and my horses, Revy and Copper. They, along with Adam, Jean, Judy, Melodee, Pam, Rikka and Paul continue to teach me to have joy and play in my life.

Lastly, thanks to the dynamic duo, Christina and Ted Winslow, publishers-extraordinaire from Big Country Publishing. They are such a joy and pleasure to play with. How did I get soooo lucky?

What else is possible beyond what we could have planned? And, thank you for the amazing YOU!!

TABLE OF CONTENTS

PART I – The Matrix

PART II – A Different Possibility

PART III

Part I
The Matrix

"Our deepest fear is not that we are inadequate.

Our deepest fear is that we are powerful beyond measure.

It is our light not our darkness that frightens us."

~Marianne Williamson

PROLOGUE

My target with sharing this story and writing this book is to show you another possibility. Perhaps to inspire you to something different - to something beyond what you knew was possible.

What if you are not wrong and have never been wrong? What if you could come out of the judgment of you and become truly grateful for you? What if you are the difference the world requires? What if you are the gift the world is waiting for just waiting to be unwrapped? Would you choose for you whatever will unlock that?

For me, the tools I'm sharing in my story from Access Consciousness™ have expanded my living beyond anything I could have imagined. This is the weirdest and wackiest modality that I have ever come across, but the tools and processes work so dynamically that I desired to share how my life has changed by applying them.

And, I know that some people may require more graphic descriptions of the abuse. In some cases, I don't have specific memories, and in other cases, I just choose to leave the details out. In any case, my intention is not to hide anything. My intention is only to facilitate greater awareness and a different possibility around abuse.

I don't claim to have any answers, only you know what works for you. So, trust what you know. And, enjoy the adventure....

~CHAPTER I ~

THE BEGINNING...

I heard the doorknob turn slowly, so slowly. My heart raced, and I held my breath. It was pitch dark, and I was waiting for the familiar shadow to appear. What will happen now? Will this be the last time? Should I scream out, "NO! Leave me alone!" Familiar body tremors took over my body as I knew this wasn't going to be the last time. Tears rolled down my cheeks as my breath shortened. How could this be happening again? Why do I have to live in fear?

This existence was all I knew. I often looked out my bedroom window and dreamed of being a happy, carefree kid playing on the swings I saw outside. Climbing on the jungle gym with careless abandon. Riding on the seesaw – up and down, up and down, up and down. Swinging on the swing so high that I thought I might touch the clouds if I dreamed hard enough. I thought to myself, "Isn't that what life should be like for a six-year-old? Shouldn't I be riding around on my bike with my friends exploring the neighborhood instead of being depressed and anxious?"

Most of my childhood I felt so sad and lonely. I would hide in my bedroom, crying for hours until my pillow was soaked. Wasn't there another possibility? Why did I choose this? Was this real? Was everyone really unhappy inside? How come it seemed like it was only me? Or, was I picking

Linda Wasil

this up from everyone around me? Everyone else *seemed* happy, but how were they *really* feeling on the inside? Behind closed doors, what was really going on? Were they living in a prison whose walls seemed insurmountable as well, but no one was talking about it?

Were most people truly unhappy trying to pretend in this make-believe world? And, was I picking up on the thoughts, feelings, and emotions of those around me? Could I actually just be aware and perceiving all of this? What if none of what I was aware of was actually mine? That was such a foreign concept at this age but I had some revelations about this later on in life....

~ Chapter II ~

Growing Up

*L*iving in this prison was suffocating, so I created an imaginary world in my mind. In this world I felt powerful and in control. I could create any situation and control the outcome. In this world I was happy and carefree. I'd be out in a magical rain forest running and playing with deer, fox, chipmunks, monkeys, and raccoons. They would tell me their secrets and where they hid at night and what they liked to eat. I would be invited to their private dens deep under the earth. It was fascinating to go on adventures with my imaginary friends. I felt special that they trusted and welcomed me as part of their family.

Playing with my dolls also brought so much joy. My imagination raced as I made up incredible adventures for Barbie and her make-believe friends. I would play for hours in the backyard hiding in the bushes by the side fence. Here, I felt safe to create in this imaginary world filled with possibility.

I created Barbie doll clothes from scraps thrown in a dumpster outside the fashion district. On Sundays my family would take a drive into downtown Boston, and we would go by the fashion district and check out our favorite dumpsters. That's where I would find fabulous scraps of upscale material, buttons, etc. that were unique and luxurious. I could sew really cool clothes that my friends envied. Coats with real fur, bell-bottom pants with sparkles, and coats with leather fringe. I was known for having the most creative and fashionably dressed Barbie in the neighborhood. Somehow through Barbie, I was able to have a sense of fitting in, though I normally felt like a misfit. I loved living my life through my dolls.

Painting was one of my favorite hobbies. I loved the oil paint-by-number kits and begged my parents to buy me one every two weeks. I would paint for hours under the willow tree in the backyard. I would glance at the sun bursting through the clouds and the birds flying by. Often I would catch the forsythia blossoms opening. The vibrant yellow buds would fill the yard with color.

The backyard was a wonderland where I could get lost. I would watch the squirrels climb the pine trees that seemed to go on forever into the sky. I wished that I could climb that high to get away from everything. One time I took a ladder and managed to reach the first limb and made it halfway up the tree. My small feet slipped on the sap, and I almost fell a couple times. Luckily, my sister was playing nearby, and I called her and she held the ladder so that I could get down safely. This was the last time I attempted to climb this tree.

~Chapter III ~

Field Trips

I was a very curious child. I loved visiting the field behind my house and took a magnifying glass and would stare at the animal tracks left in the snow or mud. I would go to the library and get books out and identify the tracks. Mostly tracks were left behind by possums, squirrels, raccoons, and fox.

There were berry bushes, lilacs, lily of the valley, big trees, and lots of wood. I would build forts in the trees and read and paint for hours. This was my wonderland and escape from the insanity of the "prison."

When we were in our teens we would sneak out there and try to pretend like grown-ups and smoke Marlboros just like the guy on the TV commercial. We thought we were so cool and it was exciting to buy cigarettes at the local five-and-dime store. How times have changed!

Most of the time we rode our bikes to get to the store. Part of the adventure was biking through a tunnel that had a very narrow sidewalk. We would wait for the coast to be clear of cars and then race through the tunnel. Adrenaline filled our bodies as we peddled faster and faster often looking back to see if a car was approaching. Sometimes we'd see a big truck approaching that seemed like it could entirely fill the tunnel!

Linda Wasil

It was worth the trip as this candy store had the best selection of one-cent candy. For less than a quarter, we left the store with a paper bag full of colorful treats. One of my favorites was a round caramel candy with sugar in the middle. I would pop out the sugary center with my finger and then eat the caramel. Yummy! We had so much fun gobbling up the candy on the way home.

Most of the time when we reached home our bags were nearly empty – and we were ready to make another trip. We divided up our allowance money so that we could go candy shopping three times a week. The official candy shopping days of each week were carefully marked on a calendar hung behind my bedroom door. As we completed each trip, we would make an "X" on the calendar. We anxiously awaited our next adventure to the candy store.

~ CHAPTER IV ~

MUSIC MANIA

*M*usic was a way that I could find joy in the otherwise difficult school years. It started with the flutophone in the second grade. I loved it and would practice for hours driving my mother crazy as I played the same songs over and over again.

In third grade my parents agreed that music would be good for me; primarily since my grandfather enjoyed musical instruments and had played the mandolin in the "old" country. They decided I should play an instrument as well so I started to play the clarinet.

Growing up I was only exposed to songs on the radio and my parent's favorite music, the polka. The symphonic nature of the songs we played in band opened up a new world for me. I would practice for hours and before long I was first row. In junior high, one of my first crushes was with a guy who was first chair. I would stare at him and dreamed about dating him all the while never having the guts to look him directly in the eye or even smile at him.

I would write about him in my journal and secretly day after day hoped that someday he would ask me out. On occasion, the band leader would have auditions to try out for another chair in the band. Since I didn't desire to upset "my crush," I purposely didn't play well in the audition even though I actually had more talent than him. It's so interesting that my crush was all in my head, a fantasy. I hardly had the courage to say "hi" to him, let alone date him.

Then, the unthinkable happened. He asked out one of my closest friends who also had a crush on him. Now I got to see them happy and holding hands at parties while I secretly dreamed that someday he and I would go out. Wow. It's amazing how in my head this fantasy seemed so real. Like I could orchestrate everything I desired and live my life through my mind and what I could make up through thinking and imagining. Little did I know that this was far from reality. Silly me!

In high school I joined the marching band. Our marching band was routinely voted the best in the state and we would practice for hours after school and have lots of fun on the football field.

I found it easy to coordinate the steps on the field with the music. I imagined the football field as a maze of lines where I was supposed to move – like a game board. This image assisted me in recalling the more complicated moves.

One year we were in an international competition and went to Bermuda to compete. I sold raffle tickets so that I could go on the trip and have my airfare paid for. Every Saturday for six weeks I went to the local Stop 'N Shop and stood for hours just outside the store selling raffle tickets.

Overall, I was amazed at how easy it was to sell the tickets. I was one of only a couple students out of about a hundred that reached their target of selling tickets before the deadline date. I recall when I sold the last ticket how happy I was. I jumped with joy and shouted, "Yes!" I accomplished this on my own, and my parents didn't have to pay anything toward the trip, because I sold all my allotted tickets. Yeah!

When we arrived in Bermuda, I looked with wonder at the tropical plants, clear blue-green water, and pure white sand. Flowers in every color of the rainbow were everywhere. Their fragrance was so strong that the wind smelled like perfume.

Buildings were painted in pastels and the streets and sidewalks were litter-free. People seemed carefree as they rode their scooters through the streets. "Wow!" I thought. "If ever there was a paradise, this is it..." I was so grateful that I was able to travel here!

We stayed in military barracks, and I was so excited that I had a hard time sleeping at night. Many nights I would sneak out of the barracks to rest on the lawn or take a walk in the moonlight. I discovered an exit route away from the security guards so I could go on my adventures unnoticed.

Staring up at the stars, I would make wishes and imaginary objects out of the stars. I took a small flashlight so that I could write in my diary and scribbled that I would like to travel more when I got older. It was so much fun to explore and learn about different cultures.

When I returned home I often thought of the magical moments in Bermuda. How I wished I could snap my fingers or wiggle my nose, and "just like that" transport back to this island of paradise. If only for a few minutes in my mind, I would be able to "get away from it all" and leave my troubles behind...

~ CHAPTER V ~

PUPPY LOVE

*M*y siblings and I loved animals and every stray animal we came across we tried to rescue. It seemed like at least twice a month a stray dog would wonder into our backyard. We would feed and care for it until the rescue league came by.

Oh, how we wished we could have adopted all of these animals! But, my sister was allergic to fur so adoption was out of the question. We still continued to beg our parents for a dog. One time my dad couldn't resist and took us to the rescue league.

We fell in love with a Labrador retriever puppy and named it Goldie for its soft, golden fur. After about one week, my sister started wheezing and getting sick from the fur, so the doctor said the puppy had to be returned.

My heart sank with the news. The puppy brought so much joy to the house. I would play with it for hours and laugh and laugh as it chased its tail. I could hear it crying at night and would get up to comfort it. I would fall asleep night after night holding it in my arms on the kitchen floor.

My mother would come out and check on me and warn me to go back to bed. I would go back to my bedroom and when my mom was asleep, sneak back out to play and comfort the puppy. I loved these quiet, tender moments caring for Goldie in the darkness.

I never cried as much as I did the day we returned Goldie. Somewhere, I gave up on my dream of being happy that stormy afternoon. I knew that someday when I was "older," I would get my own dog. One that wouldn't be taken away from me...

In the meantime, there were lots of neighbors' dogs to play with. And, a stray dog would find its way to our house at least twice a month. Alone in bed at night, I would sometimes ask if there were any dogs in need. I would promise to provide comfort and love for them if they came to me.

Many times, the day after asking for a dog in need, a stray would "appear" on our front lawn ready to be loved. I would run down the front steps and gently reach out with my hand so that the dog could smell my scent. I would wait patiently, sometimes an hour, for the dog to come toward me. It was only at this time that I would gently stroke it and tell it that everything would be okay, and I would do everything I could to assist and provide water and food. I loved comforting stray dogs – if only for a few days. It seemed like a part of me was healing as I comforted these lost animals.

~ CHAPTER VI ~

COLLEGE YEARS

I was so happy to be going off to college. Finally, I could leave my old life behind and begin a totally new chapter. I could create myself anew and create a totally different life. Or so it seemed…

The college I attended was in Western, MA and had an absolutely gorgeous campus. There were more than 30,000 undergraduates, so it was easy to blend in and meet new friends. The student body was very diverse with students from all across the country and the world.

The school's philosophy was quite liberal, and I appreciated the openness toward all races and sexual orientations. Overall, I felt as if everyone was accepted and wouldn't be judged. This allowance was much different than the narrow mindset of the town where I grew up. Finally, I was in an environment that encouraged being different, and I thrived.

Autumn was always amazing with outrageous fall foliage. I would take long walks in the woods and admire the beautiful colored leaves. I didn't have a car so I either rode my bike, walked, or took a bus to get around the huge campus. In my first year, I lived among the apple orchards in a dorm named after poets. I could hang out in the student lounge and listen to local musicians while studying. The library had a huge musical collection, and I could check out music and listen on headsets. I loved this life! There was such a sense of adventure and possibility.

I knew that if I studied hard I would have additional opportunities when I graduated. It was important that I could get out from under the financial entanglement I felt with my parents. I was so paranoid of doing poorly that I studied almost every second I wasn't in class or at other school events.

At one point toward the middle of my junior year, I knew that something had to change because I was getting burnt out with my busy schedule. I started asking questions that night about different ways to finish college. The next week I bumped into a student that was on exchange from California. I had never heard of the exchange program and my new friend explained that it allows students to attend schools all over the country and pay in-state tuition.

This sounded so fun that I decided to check it out. I ended up going to a meeting on exchange programs and decided to apply to schools in California. The process was so easy as if the universe was on my side, prodding me along to fulfill my dream. I picked three schools in Northern California and hoped for the best. A few months later, my hands shook as I opened the envelope. I was accepted to the top school that I chose! I was ecstatic. Wow! I was going to California! Yeah!

~ CHAPTER VII ~

NOT EATING TO FIT IN

I had a deep, dark secret. I was secretly starving myself. It seemed like it was the latest craze on campus. The news about anorexia came out with the recent article about the singer Karen Carpenter. I loved her songs and voice and memorized all of the lyrics from the Carpenter's Greatest Hits album.

As kids, we played that album over and over again. To me, Karen seemed so talented, happy, beautiful, and slender. My friends and I wished we could be just like her. Little did we know that she was starving herself.

Behind that beautiful smile and talent was a very tormented soul. Word got out on campus about her eating disorder and it seemed that it could be the answer to the dreaded freshman fifteen. I started to smell the unthinkable in bathrooms all around campus. Sometimes, I would hear the sounds echoing in the hallways of our dorm. It seemed like it was a huge secret on campus that no one talked about – but everyone knew was going on.

My weirdness around food started the summer of my senior year of high school. I was at my heaviest weight yet and a size 16. I had trouble fitting into my clothes and knew I had to take some drastic measures in order to lose weight before college.

Linda Wasil

The night of my high school graduation I came home after going to some parties and was really depressed. I ate three-quarters of my graduation cake that was in a large, flat pan. In the morning, my mom asked what had happened to the cake and I lied, saying that I had accidently knocked the cake over and then put it down the garbage disposal. After that, I vowed I would gain control over my eating.

Over the summer, I mostly drank Tab and ate popcorn and worked three jobs to save money for college. When I came home from work I would ride my bike for an hour up and down a hill nearby to work off the calories from the handful of popcorn I ate all day. I weighed myself each night and by the end of each week would marvel at how quickly the pounds were coming off. I was thrilled and with each passing day I ate less and less.

By the end of the summer, I had lost close to forty pounds and clothes were slightly baggy in a size ten. I wore clothes one to two sizes larger so no one really noticed how thin I was getting. It was great that I could keep this under wraps since then no one would ask me questions about my weight loss. It was the best-kept secret that summer.

Once I was at college, the food obsession continued. The buzz of the freshman fifteen was in the air. My style was to eat as little as possible and to record what foods I ate along with the calorie count. If I went over the allotted calorie count for the day, I would make it up by exercising more or by eating less the next day.

This all seemed rather "normal" since most of my friends were either dieting or watching their weight. I knew many of my classmates were anorexic and they shared their dieting secrets. Quite a few binged and purged, but I wasn't aware of the official name for bulimia at that time.

~ Chapter VIII ~

California Dreaming

*M*y last year of college in Northern California was so refreshingly different. I met new friends and got involved in student government. I rode my bike for miles every weekend exploring the countryside and almond orchards.

There was an awesome park with a rushing stream where people went tubing in the summer. They even filmed Robin Hood in this park. At dusk it felt like magic was in the air as we hiked through the deep woods. It felt like Robin and his crew were going to greet us at every turn. This park became my haven, and I started to bike and run even more.

Everything was an adventure, including trying out new restaurants and cuisine. I learned to eat avocados, hot peppers, and Mexican food. At first I couldn't remember if it was the green or the red peppers that were hot, so I frequently ended up burning the roof of my mouth. My roommate loved making guacamole and at first I couldn't stand to taste it. After a few tastes, I learned to love the creamy texture and use it for dipping. It's one of my favorite foods now.

I loved all of the beautiful flowers and the fact that everything seemed fresh and new. The buildings, roads, malls – everything was newer than on the East Coast. And, the roads weren't full of potholes!

Linda Wasil

I loved the warm, balmy summer nights with a gentle breeze. I especially appreciated the fact that there really wasn't a winter, per se. If we desired to get a "taste" of snow, we could always go to the mountains for the weekend. That sure beat trudging through the snow to get to class or freezing my butt off going across campus! Brrrrr!

~ Chapter IX ~

Post-College Dayz

Once I graduated I chose to stay in California to look for a job. I was ecstatic when I accepted my first position and moved to the Bay Area. The company paid my moving expenses and helped me find an apartment. Finally, I could really begin the adventure of building my life. However, instead of every day being an adventure, I spent most of my time working.

For many years, I poured all of my energy into my career. That's what most of my friends were doing and what was valued. After all, I lived in Silicon Valley and working long hours was the norm. I strived to be a perfectionist and put work first before anything else. People bragged about the long hours they were "putting in," often sleeping at the office.

Most of my value came from receiving promotions or accolades for my work. Finally, I had the answer for a successful life, or so I thought. I could erase my child-hood memories if I was a "success" in the corporate world. Although I was making great money and had "the title," I was miserable inside, always doubting myself and fearing that the other shoe was going to drop.

One day while driving my car in a heavy rainstorm in Northern California, I suddenly felt like I was in a trance. The windshield wipers and their motion became very present to me, as if the blades had magical-wiper powers, whispering a secret message. Back and forth, back and forth, back and forth, back and forth…whispering a message to my heart from a mystical, rain-drenched heaven.

The rain and the wipers acted as a catalyst for some kind of miracle of awareness. It was as if while whisking sheets of water away and clearing my vision to see the road, they were also giving me hidden truths about myself which came bursting from my subconscious and into the light of day. All the memories came flooding back. Memories of all those unhappy days and nights I had tried so hard to wash away by simply ignoring them.

Inside the cloud of unknowing, I saw myself: the door opening, my body trembling and all the raw, familiar scenes. I was able to pull the car over to the side of the road, my head buried in my hands as my body shook. How could I have repressed all of these memories of childhood abuse for so long? Am I dreaming? Is this real? Why was this coming up now after all of these years? Is this part of the reason for my unshakable depression and lack of will to live? What do I do now? How will I sleep? Is there anyone I can confide in?

~ Chapter X ~

Therapy

*T*he next week I started intensive therapy. At first, I couldn't even speak. The body trembling continued as each memory, before exiting my body, left with an earth-quake-type tremor. I cried until my sides hurt. How could I talk about all of this? It all seemed jumbled in my mind. Was it really true or was I making it up?

Slowly, over weeks and months, words replaced tears. Every week I dove deeper and deeper into the darkness. Nothing seemed to stop the endless depression and hopelessness. My therapist suggested medication to ease the pain. I refused to fill the prescription, desiring to be present to every emotion and feeling coming up from inside of me.

Over and over again my therapists had said that I was the victim of what had occurred to me. That I had been powerless throughout it all. I really believed what they were telling me. Why would I believe anything otherwise? This is what society says, that we're "victims" of abuse. That I was a victim to and had been victimized by the abuse. That it was a terrible wrongness and should never have happened. "So," I thought, "this is great...I get to be a victim and that's the reason why I'm unhappy with my life and why I can't create something different." I blamed everything on the abuse.

Linda Wasil

Somewhere, I also felt that I had caused it, that otherwise it never would have happened. This created tremendous guilt and a conflict in my universe as I blamed myself again and again for what had occurred. It really had been my fault. Somehow I had been too needy or too sexual or something else. The questions were like an endless loop.

Years passed and I progressed into more intensive treatment programs. Pounding pillows and recounting my story seemed to make things worse at times. Was this pain ever going to end? None of this seemed to help much as I was just replaying the story over and over again. It was a relief to be heard initially, but I desired something more. I continued searching...

I read and studied every self-help book I could get my hands on. I took intensive weekend courses that gave me a temporary "high" that lasted a few days then stumbled back into hopelessness and depression. Again, I didn't understand why I was still feeling this way. After all, I owned a beautiful house in the Bay Area, had two cars, took luxury vacations, had a great job and friends, made great money, yet I still had these negative feelings and self-doubt.

One day, as I looked out into the rays of sun through the pine trees in my newly landscaped backyard, I said to the universe, "If things don't change, I'm outta here, and I mean it! You have one month to show me a different path, or I'm leaving this planet for good."

~ Chapter XI ~

The Turning Point

*T*he very next day I was in my kitchen ironing when I received an intuitive message to turn on the radio to an AM station. What? I never listened to the radio in the house and, if I did, I listened to FM. Yet the knowing was so strong, I didn't doubt it this time.

I quickly walked over to the stereo and turned the radio on. My fingers stopped at a station where I heard a man speaking about verbal clearings and energy work that could transform any area of your life that wasn't working. Even though this sounded too easy, I kept listening. He talked about asking questions to unlock limitations. This process, he said, allowed people to have an awareness of what is true for them. The work was called Access Consciousness™.

For example, he spoke about one of his clients who was unhappy in her marriage of twenty-five years, but unable to leave her husband. She had recently been diagnosed with breast cancer and was going to begin chemotherapy. Through a series of questions, he helped her to see that she had created the cancer as a way out of her marriage. When she became aware of this, she made the choice to leave her husband.

Linda Wasil

As he recalled numerous successes with clients, for the first time in a very long while, I felt excitement and my body was at ease. I called into the radio program and asked a question on the air and booked a session the next day. I wondered, "Could this be what I had been asking for?"

Over the course of several weeks, all of the stories that had been locked inside me started to unravel. I felt lighter and the depression started to lift. At one point, the facilitator asked me a question about my childhood that blew my mind: What if I knew everything that was going to happen in my childhood before I was even born?

What?! Instantly I felt lighter, but a part of me didn't want to believe I actually chose my family situation. What a bizarre concept! It took a while to sink in, but there was something to this. Just this question alone started to unravel something inside me.

He paused and continued, "What if I chose this because I knew I was strong enough to survive it and it may have prevented someone else from being abused?" I felt lighter when he asked this question, but I didn't hear any sounds, I only watched his lips move. He explained that whatever made me feel lighter was true and heavier was a lie. He had to repeat the question three times before I could begin to hear it. On the fourth try, I was able to hear the entire question. And, when I finally heard it, it unraveled something deep down in my core and my body felt much calmer. All of this time I had bought the lie that I was a victim. If I chose this, could this mean I was actually a powerful being instead of a victim?

This awareness shook my very core. I had played the victim role so well and it had served me in many ways. Could all of this self-doubt and sadness be a cover-up for the potency and joy that I truly am? This seemed almost unthinkable, but somehow I knew this was true.

Even though the facilitator was bringing up some totally out-of-the-box concepts that sounded totally insane at times, I continued having private sessions. These concepts were almost the opposite of what I had been exposed to in traditional therapy, but they were working. Instead of rehashing the story and getting in touch with my feelings like in traditional therapy, I was able to unlock what was trapped in my body and release what wasn't working anymore through questions.

These sessions began to unlock the twisted web of lies that I had bought into. Lies I had bought from myself, friends, society, and my therapists. Finally, I started to trust that I was on the path to breaking free from the lies I had bought into.

Somehow, the questions were opening me up to new awarenesses. Things began to shift dynamically. I felt lighter and my life started to get easier and more fun. As the layers peeled away, I started to see where I had chosen abuse in my life.

For instance, I realized that I had been addicted to work, food, abusive relationships, etc., to dull the pain and check out. I started the journey of asking questions to unlock these areas in my life where I felt stuck.

~ CHAPTER XII ~

ENDING AN ABUSIVE RELATIONSHIP

I began to see that I was in an abusive relationship with my boyfriend that had slowly eroded my self-esteem. It's interesting that when we first started dating, I would sense that his comments weren't kind, but I didn't say anything because I believed deep down that I didn't deserve to be treated any better. On the rare occasion that I would stand up for myself and state that I didn't appreciate his sarcastic comments, he would tell me that it was all in my head and that I was being too sensitive.

Over time, his cutting remarks would be coupled with pinching or slapping. Even if I asked him to stop, he would continue until I was in tears. When I showed him the bruises on my body, he would deny that he caused them and claimed that again I was "too sensitive."

One night as we were arguing, he twisted my arm as he threatened me. With tears running down my cheeks, I begged him to stop as the pain in my shoulder intensified. Eventually, he let me go when I promised to never raise my voice to him again. That evening with an ice pack on my shoulder, I held myself in a fetal position as I tried to sleep. My mind raced as I replayed the events of the evening.

The next morning, my boyfriend apologized and said that he didn't mean anything by his threats and wouldn't hurt me again. This time I didn't believe him and knew that I had to leave. The violence was clearly escalating. More importantly, as I started to value myself I KNEW that I deserved better. I made a demand to never be in an abusive relationship again, and with that I ended the relationship. I had finally had enough.

~ CHAPTER XIII ~

SEARCHING FOR MR. WRONG

*S*o much of my life I had felt "wrong" for not being in a relationship. This especially came up around the holidays and so-called "date nights" each week. Eating alone at restaurants, people would stare at me. I could read their minds. People would question – is she a loner, recently separated, difficult to be around, or does she not like people? How about, it's far easier to be with myself instead of in a relationship that doesn't work?! You see, my girlfriends and I would joke about BTN's – better-than-nothing relationships. How many times had I stayed in a relationship that wasn't working just to "fit in?"

It seemed like the times I had a relationship, all of the sudden I "fit in." I would get invited to dinner parties and over to people's houses "if" (this being the key word) I had a boyfriend. People, practically strangers, would ask how "the relationship" was going. All of a sudden we had something to talk about, to commiserate about. Having a relationship was like a magic ticket – a ticket to be accepted into society. I was suddenly cast as a "success" as long as I had a relationship. People became interested in me and my relationship. Without one, I was an outcast. I perceived the judgments.

Why would anyone choose to be alone? It didn't make sense in most people's eyes. So I attempted to fit in by staying in relationships that just plain didn't work. I would choose men that were "fixer uppers" and spend all of my time and energy trying to "fix" them. That way I didn't have to look at the problems in my life.

Even if the guy was somewhat abusive, I would stay in the relationship. After all, there had to be a reason that my boyfriend was acting that way. Perhaps he had been scarred by a horrible childhood, had been neglected, and abused. I realized over time that people can choose to be mean and abusive – they don't require a reason to act the way they do. Oftentimes, it's challenging to become aware of this.

I didn't desire to see that people could be mean because they chose it. I always looked at the good in people and was blindsided by the mean things they would do – just for the fun of it. I couldn't wrap my brain around that one. Why would anyone like to purposely hurt another person? Because they can. Because they can. Because they can. What? Repeat. Because they can. What? Repeat. BECAUSE THEY CAN. They don't require a reason. There didn't have to be a justification.

Wow! That totally blew my mind apart. You mean I could choose to be mean and to purposely hurt someone else? What?! That had never entered my mind. It slowly started to sink in as I was able to observe how certain men in my life had treated me. I realized I had to be aware of the good, the bad, and the ugly in people.

As I came out of judgment of the wrongness of me, I was able to become more aware of this. And, as I continued to move into gratitude for myself, I began to choose differently. Yeah! Choice creates awareness. Awesome! I didn't have to choose the same "type" of men anymore. How can it get any better than this?

PART II
A Different Possibility:
Using the Tools from
Access Consciousness™

*What if nothing you've ever done
in your life was wrong?
What if every point of view was just
an interesting point of view?
What if everything about me that I've
considered a wrongness is actually
a strongness?
What if everything is the opposite
of what it appears to be?
What's right about me that
I'm not getting?*

With infinite gratitude to Gary Douglas,
founder of Access Consciousness™

~ CHAPTER XIV ~

BEYOND VICTIM

*O*ne of the turning points for me was when I had the awareness that I chose the sexual abuse in order to protect my sister from experiencing it. What? This seemed so strange. How could that be? How could someone so young and small choose this? I was just an innocent kid, or was I?! How could little old (young) me actually choose something like this?

At first, it seemed utterly insane. My mind raced back and forth over all of the memories and what I had hidden deep down inside the very core of me. Things I had hidden even from myself. And, it turned how I felt about myself upside down and inside out!

You see, I probably could have won an Academy Award for playing the victim. If the right people had been watching, I could have been a twenty-five time nominee for best dramatic actress for my stunning and moving performances of the powerless, pathetic woman with the great heart who so longs to sees the good that surely must be in all people. Right?! It was the longest running role in my life. Playing this role, I could continue to hide and keep myself small. The victim role was also useful in controlling others. With just the right twist of the story and a few tears,

I had people feeling sorry for me. Somewhere I loved this. I came to realize that. I loved playing the victim role, it served a purpose! I felt powerful and in control in this role.

I was able to get lots of sympathy telling the drama and trauma stories about what wasn't working in my life. I could go on and on with the pain and agony of how awful and depressing my life was. Do you hear the violins playing in the background? People really seemed to relate to these stories and tried to comfort me. Oh poor, pitiful me! Ha! It seemed like most people liked it when I was anxious and unhappy – almost if they could relate to me more when I was sad.

Being a victim also meant that I didn't have to take responsibility for what I was creating in my life. I could blame what I wasn't happy with on what "happened" in the past. How could I move beyond this with all the pain and suffering I had endured? Again, do you hear the violins playing? I was continuously referencing the past and replaying the scenes in my head. It was like a loop playing the same scenes over and over and over and over again. I was never able to move forward, I was stuck continuously referencing the past.

By keeping myself small, I got to continue to stay where I was and not create a joyful life. I could continue to doubt myself and blame everyone and everything for what wasn't working in my life. It was as though I didn't believe a happy life was possible. As long as I wallowed in the sadness, I couldn't get past it. At some point, I said enough is enough! I'm done with this. This really isn't working for me! I'm choosing something different today!

~ CHAPTER XV ~

THE TRUTH OF ME

*W*ith the awareness that I had actually chosen the abuse, it was impossible to view myself as a victim any longer. I came to realize that I was WAY stronger than I ever thought possible. It really turned everything upside down as this was the complete opposite of how I had been viewing myself. Finally, I could break free of this cycle!

As I had more awarenesses, I realized that I actually KNEW what was going to happen. Therefore, I was a master manipulator in stopping it from happening to someone else. I was actually able to perceive the future! When I had this awareness, it felt so light. It was like a huge weight had been lifted from my shoulders. All of these years I kept wallowing in the heaviness of a lie that I thought was true – that I was a powerless, impotent, victim. Ha! Was that a big, ol', fat lie?!

So, how many of you like me have bought that you are a victim of abuse? Everything that is, will you destroy and uncreate it? (This will start to unlock the energy around this.)

As I started to tap into the energy of who I truly be, I realized the tremendous strength, courage, and awareness that I had as a small child. I had cut off my strength, because I had bought the lie that I was powerless. Silly me!

By continuing to ask questions, I was able to get myself out of the web of lies that seemed to strangle my very existence.

Over time, all of this began to make more and more sense. After all, I had spent years and years attempting to figure out the abuse in therapy. Trying to get to the root of why this "happened" to me. Somehow I thought I could get past it by understanding why this had "happened." So, I had gone to private therapy, group therapy, outpatient hospital groups, and motivational workshops to figure this out. But nothing had seemed to work or have a lasting effect. I had still felt depressed and kept searching for something that could actually create the change I was looking for.

When I started to ask questions using the Access™ tools, things really started to shift. Once I had the awareness of the true strength of me and that I had actually chosen the abuse, everything started to unlock. There was such a lightness to the fact that I was actually extremely strong and courageous. There was a lightness to my being that I had NEVER experienced pounding pillows in therapy.

I realized the anger was a lie. It was actually the potency that was underlying everything that desired to get out. A potency that could be a catalyst for change. A potency that I could tap into to create and generate a joyful, abundant, and ease-filled life.

As I attended more classes, it was actually quite common that the so-called victims had actually chosen the abuse for different reasons. Some had chosen it to protect others, some to get back at the abuser from another lifetime, or some "victims" had been abusers in the past. Whatever the case may be, as these awarenesses came to light, each person got to look at the fact that they had actually chosen the abuse. Then, they had a choice to break free of the victim program that they had been running. I'm not saying that this is true for everyone so follow what YOU know is true for you.

My hope in sharing this is if you have a similar story or if you feel stuck, that you start asking questions to unlock and provide clarity on whatever is holding the "stuckness" in place. If there is a "stuckness," perhaps there is a lie somewhere holding all of that in place? So, you may start by asking the following questions:

What information do I require

to have clarity with this?

Is there a lie here that's holding this in place?

What is the lie here that I'm buying?

Did I choose this?

Did I have something to do with creating this?

What did I choose this for?

What is the purpose of creating this abuse?

What can I do to change it?

What if you are potent beyond measure, but have been seeing yourself as a victim? Would that cause some conflict in your world? It certainly did for me!

I'm going to share some Access™ tools that I've used to get out of this cycle of abuse. Use what works for you and discard what feels heavy. Continue to trust that you know what works for you! I don't have any answers. I'm only sharing what worked for me. Follow what YOU know. And, I'm so grateful that you're still reading this. I know it may seem difficult and hopeless at times, I can totally relate to that! But, if you can continue to read, you may find some of the tools life-changing. I'm grateful for the beautiful being you be. So, it's your choice my amazing friend!

~ Chapter XVI ~

A Different Possibility

*B*efore we go onto the following exercise, I'd like to ask you a question: Is your body inside you or are you inside your body? Look for the outside edges of you. Can you find them or are they everywhere? Are you getting that the outside edges are everywhere? That's correct. Your body is inside "you," the infinite being.

Now I'd like you to take a moment and find a quiet, private space. Take a few slow, deep breaths from the top of your head down to the tips of your little toes. Now take another deep breath and start to expand out to the size of the room you're in. Now continue to expand out to the entire structure that you're in including the earth, the city block, your town, your state, your country, and to the galaxies. Continue to expand out. There's not a wrong or a right way to do this exercise. Just trust that when you ask you're already becoming the space that you've asked for.

From this space, ask yourself: What's right about me that I'm not getting? Does that make you feel lighter? Remember, whatever makes you feel lighter is true for you. Whatever makes you feel heavier is a lie. So again, ask yourself: What's right about me that I'm not getting? Do you feel more like yourself after you ask this question? Do you have more space and ease?

I encourage you to ask further questions around this so that you can begin to get out of the wrongness of you into having an awareness of what's right about you. Isn't it fun to ask: What's right about me? Doesn't that make you feel lighter? What's right about me? What's right about me that I'm not getting? Play with this. What's right about me? I do this when I'm skipping and jumping around with my dog Coco. Have fun with it!

If you have some awarenesses with this, take a moment and write them down on the space below. Continue to add to this list and play with this. Look at this list often and really take in what's right about you!

_____

_____

_____

_____

_____

Are you actually much stronger and more potent than you're giving yourself credit for? Trust what YOU know. Don't trust me or anyone else. Trust yourself. You know what feels light and what feels heavy. So give yourself some space to truly get straight with what is true for you. Don't discard yourself! Really, if you've read this much of the book, some part of what I've shared must be resonating with you. You are truly a gift to the world. I'm so grateful that you've read this far. Thank you, thank you! How did I get so lucky?

One of my favorite phrases is from Gary called the crazy phrase. It may be helpful to run this at this point. What if everything is the opposite of what it appears to be and nothing is the opposite of what it appears to be? Try repeating that phrase and you won't be able to think. So, let's repeat it five times.

> *What if everything is the opposite of what it appears to be and nothing is the opposite of what it appears to be?*

> *What if everything is the opposite of what it appears to be and nothing is the opposite of what it appears to be?*

> *What if everything is the opposite of what it appears to be and nothing is the opposite of what it appears to be?*

> *What if everything is the opposite of what it appears to be and nothing is the opposite of what it appears to be?*

> *What if everything is the opposite of what it appears to be and nothing is the opposite of what it appears to be?*

How do you feel? A little spacey? Can you think? I love to use this question when I keep looping over and over on the same thought or when I'm just not feeling like myself. The question helps unlock whatever we're stuck in. It's one of my favorites!

Linda Wasil

Here's a clearing from Access™ that you may desire to run to get some clarity at this point:

What energy, space, and consciousness can me and my body be that would allow us to have total clarity and ease with all of this? Everything that doesn't allow that, will you destroy and uncreate it?

~ CHAPTER XVII ~

-◄─►--

WHO DOES THIS BELONG TO?

*T*his is an amazing, life-changing tool… What if 98% of your thoughts, feelings, and emotions don't belong to you? Does that make you feel lighter? Would that make your life a bit easier?

Since we're all psychic, we pick up on every thought, feeling, and emotion within a thousand miles or more. So how many of you have made the thoughts, feelings, and emotions you perceive real and made them yours?

As a child, I was extremely aware of everyone else's "stuff" and took it on as mine. Yikes! Since practically everyone around me was depressed, angry, anxious, etc., I thought that I was depressed, angry, and anxious too! And that's how it played out.

I slowly began to realize that as a highly aware child, all of those days I spent crying I was actually crying for everyone around me. How was I supposed to know differently? All I knew was that all of these emotions were so intense at times that I concluded that they had to be mine. I wasn't able to distinguish what was mine and what was everyone else's. And, since most of the grown-ups around me seemed to be unhappy, it didn't seem that abnormal that I would be too. I just wished that I could be happy like the young kids that were around me.

So, it was a HUGE surprise when I started using Gary's tool, "Who does this belong to?" I discovered just how much of what I was aware of actually wasn't mine! It didn't seem possible at first, but as I continued to ask this question, I realized that almost 100% of what I thought was mine was actually someone else's.

The way you use this tool is to ask, "Who does this belong to?" for every thought, feeling, and emotion you're aware of for three days. If you ask this question and things lighten up, then it's not yours. So return it to sender with consciousness attached by saying, "return to sender."

How much of what we think we're feeling, thinking, etc. is not ours? We're just psychic sponges and are picking up on every thought, feeling, and emotion within miles.

Using this tool can make us a walking meditation where we're not buying the thoughts, feelings, and emotions of others as our own.

To begin using this tool, you may just try using it for fifteen – twenty minutes at a time. Then take a break and start to use it again. It can feel like hard work, but it's worth it! The peace, ease, and empty head at the end of the three days is amazing.

Within a short period of time, you'll start to realize that almost none of the thoughts, feelings, and emotions that you've believed to be yours are actually yours. You've just been picking up on them from everyone around you.

Did you ever play the telephone game growing up, sometimes known as "Chinese Whispers?" The way it works is that someone whispers something into your ear and then you relay it to the next person, and so on and so forth, person by person until by the last person it's a totally different message. That's what happens when you take on others' thoughts as your own. Interesting, huh?

~ Chapter XVIII ~

Five Steps to Change Anything

This section is reprinted with permission from Dr. Dain Heer's book, *Being You, Changing the World*

*H*ere are some dynamic tools that I've used to create a joyful life and change whatever wasn't working in my life.

1. Make a Demand

One of the first steps for change is to make a demand such as, "No matter what it takes my life is going to change!" Or, an example from my life in response to the abusive relationship, "Enough is enough! This is stopping NOW!" That's a demand.

For me, somewhere I knew that the relationship wasn't working, but I wasn't willing to demand that it change. So I just allowed things to stay as they were. When I got to the point where I said, "Enough is enough, this is changing NOW!" things really changed quickly. I ended the relationship and never looked back.

2. Ask a Question

Every question you ask opens up a completely different possibility and a new potential.

You're making a demand and then you ask a question such as, "What's it going to take for this to show up differently?" This allows the energy of the universe to open up doorways that you never saw before. You couldn't see them until you made the demand and asked the question. Allow the universe to show you these doorways. More on asking questions in the next chapter.

3. Destroy and Uncreate

OK, so this next section may seem a bit weird...no, a LOT weird to some people. I'd like you to trust me on this and at least finish reading this section. This information really helped me change what wasn't working in my life. So, here we go. Whenever you're willing to destroy and uncreate and let go of something that is limiting you, it automatically and instantly opens up the space for something less limited or even unlimited to show up. You see, when you let go of the limited, the unlimited finally has a space to exist.

So ask yourself, "am I willing to do this?" If you get a yes, what do you have to lose? Everything you are willing to give up, uncreate, and destroy opens up to a totally different possibility in your life. So why not try it and go on the adventure?

You can never give up what you Be. Your very Being is indestructible. You can only let go of, uncreate, and destroy what is defining you, limiting you, and keeping you and your being stuck. Whenever you do this, it makes room for something different and greater to show up. Ask to destroy and uncreate and let go of everything you've created or bought as real that doesn't allow what you asked for to show up as soon as possible.

This next part is even a bit weirder. You may also choose to add the clearing statement: Right and wrong, good and bad, POC and POD, all nine, shorts, boys, and beyonds™* (or just "POC and POD all that!" for short).

Here's some clearings that you may desire to run to get some clarity at this point:

What energy, space, and consciousness can me and my body be that would allow us to have total clarity and ease with all of this? Everything that doesn't allow that, will you destroy and uncreate it? Right and wrong, good and bad, POC and POD, all nine, shorts, boys, and beyonds™.

What am I refusing to be and receive, that if I actually did be and receive, would change all realities and non-realities and manifest as the joy, strength, and possibility I truly be? Everything that doesn't allow that, will you destroy and uncreate it? Right and wrong, good and bad, POC and POD, all nine, shorts, boys and beyonds™.

You can check this out just for fun. If not, that's okay. I hope that you continue reading because I have some other tools I'd like to share.

* A further explanation of the Clearing Statement is in the back of the book in the Glossary section if you'd like to learn more.

4. Choose and Act

One of our greatest capacities as a being is the capacity to choose. Your choice actually creates a different potential for the future.

What I used to do is if I made a choice I had to stick with it – I couldn't or wouldn't allow myself to choose again. It was as if this choice was going to handle everything. Interesting, isn't it?

What I also used to do is choose only the good (right) things and not the bad (wrong) things. That takes a lot of judgment of me. What if there were no judgment? What if it was just, "Cool, I made this choice. If it works out well, I'll choose more of that. And if it doesn't work out so well… I'll just choose again!" What if there's no wrongness or rightness? No judgment? No beating yourself up if things don't work out so well? What if you could choose from the lightness? For the fun of it? Would that make it easier to choose if you knew you could choose again ten seconds later? Would that take the significance off of choosing?

So let's play with this. If you had only ten seconds to live the rest of your life, what would you choose? Now, that ten seconds is over. Choose again. And choose again for the next ten seconds. And again. How was that? Was it fun? Did you struggle some? When I first heard this exercise, I could only come up with three things, and I chose to repeat one thing twice because I couldn't come up with anything else. Funny huh?! Now, after practicing with this tool regularly, it's a lot easier to choose in ten second increments. Have fun with this and play with it! There's no right or wrong. Just choice.

Once you've made a choice, you have to act when it's necessary. One question that I use every day to assist me in knowing what actions to take is, "What can I be, do, create, and generate today that will allow this to show up right away?"

The other cool thing about choice is that choice creates awareness, not the other way around. One of the best examples I can give you on this is when I was dating the guy I mentioned earlier that was emotionally and physically abusive. At one point, when my boyfriend's abuse escalated to beyond what I thought I could handle, I had to say, "enough!" After he jokingly twisted my arm behind my back while mocking me as I pleaded for him to stop, I made a choice in that moment that I was "out of there." The next morning, I packed up all of my stuff and moved out of the house. I sneaked out after he left for work. That was really a demand that enough was enough! No more! I became clear that this wasn't working for me and that the violence was escalating. I wasn't willing to stay in the situation any more. I cared about me more than my addiction to staying in this abusive situation.

When I made the choice to leave, I started to have awarenesses of how I was treated during the relationship. I didn't fully realize how much I chose to be abused during the relationship until I made the choice to leave.

So, choice creates awareness, awareness doesn't create choice.

5. Receive Everything

For things to change, you have to be willing to receive everything that shows up with no judgment or exclusion. You have to be willing to trust the universe. You are not in control. The universe is aware of infinite possibilities

– beyond anything you could plan. So what you ask for may take awhile, but don't make yourself wrong for this. Just trust that what you've asked for is on its way, even if it takes more than ten years to receive it. And from personal experience, it seems to always look completely different than what I could have planned.

So start demanding change, ask questions, be willing to let go of your limitations, choose something different, and then act. And be patient and willing to receive everything that shows up without judgment.

~ Chapter XIX ~

Question Everything

*W*hen I was little, I was so curious and interested in lots of things that I asked my dad all kinds of questions continuously. That drove him crazy. Most of the time he didn't have an answer for my questions and made something up. I knew that he was just trying to get me to shut up, but I kept pressing for something more. At this point, he would raise his voice and tell me not to ask any more dumb questions.

Over time, I asked less and less questions. And at one point, I made a decision not to ask any more questions just to get back at my father. I also learned in school that the most important thing was to have the right answer, not to question things. I learned to shut up and figure out what the right or acceptable answer was.

I had looked for the RIGHT answer most of my life through my mind. My mind would incessantly search for the RIGHT answer. That way, I felt I had CONTROL over everything. That way I would do well in school, at my job, and make my family proud.

Well, I found that the way out of the right answer universe was to ASK A QUESTION. I had to relearn to ask questions. It seemed so strange at first and it's taken a lot of practice for me to ask questions. Here's how it works...

Once you decide on the direction you're going, you can't see any other path. You'll never be aware of other possibilities if you don't ask a question. If you ask, "What else is possible here that I haven't considered?" this opens the door to infinite possibilities.

After I had this awareness, I started asking questions about EVERYTHING! I began to see that my point of view was creating my reality and that I couldn't see any other possibilities without asking a question.

Here are some questions you can ask to open up more possibilities in your life:

How does it get any better than this? (Ask this when something "good" happens or when something "bad" happens.)

What's right about this that I'm not getting?

What would it take to change this?

What else is possible?

What would it take for this to turn out better than I could have planned?

Who am I today and what grand and glorious adventures am I going to have?

Don't start looking for the answer, please!

Here's how it usually works in this reality: We ask a question and then we go into our mind. We ask, "Is that the right answer? Is this the right answer? Is that the right answer?" Back and forth, back and forth...

The key is to ask a question and then to not look for AN ANSWER. Ask the question and go quiet for a moment and let the energy pervade your universe. This may take an hour…a day…or a month…or longer. Just let the energy pervade your universe. Not a RIGHT answer – an energy.

You see, whenever you ask a question, an energy "comes up." The energy makes itself known to you. The question opens the door to getting the energy, which will guide you to the thing for which you are asking.

So, let's play with some questions:

What gift are you to the world that you haven't acknowledged?

What's right about you that you're not getting?

What contribution are you to everyone and everything in your life that you're not acknowledging?

What contribution can you be to the earth?

What contribution from the earth are you refusing that you truly could be using to expand your life?

What ease are you refusing that you truly could be choosing to make your life a whole lot more fun?

What else is possible that you haven't even considered?

Now, be quiet and don't LOOK for an answer...

~ CHAPTER XX ~

CHOOSING GRATITUDE: GETTING OUT OF THE WRONGNESS

*H*ow many of you judge yourself nonstop? 24/7? It seems like most people do. I certainly did and have to catch myself when I start hearing the negative self-talk. What's really assisted me in getting out of this wrongness is getting up each morning and writing down three things I'm grateful for. It could be something you're grateful for about you, your life, someone in your life, your pet, etc. It's something I look forward to each morning and joyfully wake up and have my Gratitude Journal by my nightstand. Right now, take a moment and write down three things you're grateful for.

I'm grateful for these three things:

_____

_____

_____

Now, close your eyes and take a deep breath. How do you feel after writing these three things down? Do you feel lighter? Whatever makes you feel lighter is true for you and whatever makes you feel heavier is a lie.

What's interesting about having gratitude is that you can't have gratitude and judgment at the same time. Isn't that awesome?! You can't have gratitude and judgment at the same time!

Another question I love asking, which I referenced in an earlier chapter is, "What's right about me that I'm not getting?"

So ask, "What's right about me?"

Asking what's right about this or right about me can be so liberating. It's like a breath of fresh air to a different possibility. Asking this opens up the gates to something completely different. Instead of focusing on what's wrong with you, asking, "What's right about me that I'm not getting?" is really liberating. It's like all of the sudden a lightbulb goes off and you start focusing on what's "cool" about you.

Everyone has unique talents and abilities and asking this question takes us out of the wrongness that so many of us choose. Try asking the question, "What's right about me?" when you're feeling a little wonky or when you're not smiling. Ask any time and see how the energy shifts. I have a post-it note in my car with this question on it. It brings a smile to my face every time I see it!

What's right about me that I'm not getting? Repeat. What's right about me that I'm not getting? Does that make you feel lighter? Again, if you do, then you know it's true!

~ CHAPTER XXI ~

WHO ARE YOU? FINDING THE ENERGY OF YOU...

*I*f no one ever teaches you how to be, how can you step into an awareness of what it's like to be you? When I first heard this, I was like, "What? The energy of me? What is THAT?!" It seemed like that was such a foreign concept to me since I was always trying to fit into what other people expected of me.

This was especially the case growing up. I was painfully shy and really desired to be liked and to have friends. To fit in, I recalled how I would duplicate how the "cool" kids in the neighborhood acted and dressed. I would make jokes and tell lies that really made me feel uncomfortable.

The popular kids talked a lot about others and were generally mean to those that were considered different. I desperately desired to fit in, but I knew it was fruitless. I ended up disliking myself even more by trying to duplicate others. And I didn't enjoy being mean to the kids that were classified as outcasts.

At some point, I chose to leave the group and befriend the outcasts. The popular kids had pity on me, but I didn't care. I wasn't having fun being someone that I wasn't, and I couldn't be mean to those that were considered different. I had totally divorced me to fit in, but I still wasn't sure what it was like to be me.

One thing that assisted me in finding the energy of me was to look at times in the past when I had no judgment, no thought, total peace, and a joy in just being. These were also times that I had a sense of possibility and exuberance. Those were the times when I was being me.

Here are some examples from my life:

I used to love to explore in the field behind my house growing up. Being in nature was a place of no judgment and total beauty. The space to truly be me and explore. I would go out to the field every day after school and spent most weekends exploring in the woods. I would read countless books on wild animals and how to identify their footprints. I would find footprints in the wet sand by the stream or after a rain shower. When I found a footprint, I would take out my trusty field guide and my magnifying glass and identify the print.

Most of the time the prints were from a raccoon, squirrel, rabbit, or possum. One time, I was so excited to identify a fox print. I desired so desperately to see the fox that I would sneak out of my house at night and wait by the back fence with a flashlight. I would setup a makeshift tent made out of an old blanket and a cardboard box. I would stare up at the stars and wait for any movement so that I could shine my flashlight in hopes of catching a glimpse of the fox. I never did see the fox, but heard many creatures moving in the bushes under the moonlight.

Spending time in the field exploring was truly a joyful and peaceful time for me. I would giggle in wonderment at the beautiful wild lilac bushes and lily of the valley scattered throughout the field. When there was a strong wind, I would position myself so that the scent of the lilacs would stream by with such intensity that I felt I could be knocked over by the yumminess of the smell. I would eat handfuls of wild blueberries, blackberries, and strawberries and pretend I could live off of the land. I built many small huts throughout the field where I would bring a book and write in my journal in total peace.

One of my favorite huts was high up in a pine tree, and I would marvel at the sap streaming down the side of the tree. The pine cones on this tree were also so large that when they dropped to the ground they would make a deep thunk and bounce. Sometimes I would climb down to explore the pine cones and would marvel at the tiny seeds nestled in each cone. I would keep my favorite pine cones stashed in a wooden bowl on my bureau in my bedroom. The pine smelled so wondrous and filled my room with fragrance. The woods were truly a sanctuary for me, and I so appreciated the many gifts present in the trees and in this field.

This field was truly a place where I could go to be totally at peace and joyful. I would write about different adventures or possibilities I could choose. Anything felt possible with nature. Anything... There was an exuberance in my being from being in nature, a sense of space, and so much gratitude for being.

I hope that these examples from my life will assist you in identifying times in your life when you were truly being you. These were times when you were totally at peace, had no judgment, and had a sense of joy in being alive.

Linda Wasil

Write down three examples and, if you have more, keep on writing. Take out a separate sheet of paper if required. Don't think about it too much. Just start writing.

1. _____

_____

_____

2. _____

_____

_____

3. _____

_____

_____

~ Chapter XXII ~

Choosing for Me

When I first was asked what "choosing for me" would look like, I went blank. What the heck did that mean? I had no idea what choosing for me would even look like! It seemed like such a foreign concept. That's what went through my mind when I heard the question, "Linda, what would you choose if you were choosing for YOU?"

I reflected on this question for many months, and it's taken years to become clearer on what choosing for me would look like... (And I'm still becoming more aware of this!). When I sat down and really looked at this, I realized how many of my choices in life I had chosen for someone or something else...my family, friends, boyfriend, boss, neighbors, the church, etc. I had never really even looked at what would work for me or even have me in the computation! Ha, that's funny isn't it?! No wonder I wasn't happy with many of the choices I made. I wasn't really living my life; I was living a life that seemed to work for everyone else...except ME!

So I started to ask the question, "If I was living the life I truly desire, what would that look like?" I got a pad of paper and started to look at what it was that I desired in my life.

Take a few moments to jot down some notes in response to this question on a separate piece of paper or use the space below. And if you like, destroy and uncreate everything that doesn't allow this to be easy. This will be helpful to look at before the next chapter, which really looks into getting the life and living you truly desire.

_____

_____

_____

_____

_____

_____

_____

_____

~ Chapter XXIII ~

Getting the Living You Truly Desire

*H*ow many of you are totally happy with your life as it is? How many of you don't have any idea what you want to do, but you just know you need to change the way you are living? I know that I wasn't totally happy with my life. There were aspects of my life that were joyful and aspects that were not working so great. I just wasn't sure how to change things. To help me get clear on what I would like to have as my life, I used a really cool tool called "the energy ball exercise."

The energy ball exercise from Access Consciousness™ is a totally different way of inviting what you'd like your life to be. It's a way of asking and receiving from the infinite universe by speaking its language – the language of energy.

You see, over the years I took lots of visualization workshops where I would create a collage from pictures I cut out of magazines of what I desired in my life. I would look at the pictures and put my desire "out there" in order to create it.

This method never really seemed to work for me consistently. It seemed like I was trying to control or even limit what I could create. It wasn't as effective as the energy ball exercise, which opened me up to the energy of what

Linda Wasil

I desired to create my life as. This allowed the universe to show me infinite possibilities around the energy of what I was asking to be created. It was a totally different way of inviting what I'd like as my life to be.

Here are the steps for the energy ball exercise and further explanation will be provided.

Creating Your Energy Ball

1. Ask, "What would I like my life to look like and be like?" Get the energy of that and put it out in front of you.

2. Pull energy into it from all over the universe and let little trickles go out to all those people who are looking for you and don't know it.

3. Anything that shows up in your life that FEELS like the energy you described in step 1, whether it makes sense to you or not, go do it. Follow that energy.

Step 1

What I did was write down the elements of what I would like to have as my life. I asked, "If there were no limitations in my world regarding time, money, creative and generative capacities, what would I ask for? What would I choose right away?" I got the way it would feel to have all of those things showing up.

For instance, I desired a new place in which I'd love to live. I didn't go into the specifics like, "I'd like a three-bedroom/two-bathroom home with a fenced yard on a corner lot." I got the way I would feel to have a place in which I'd love to live.

For relationships, I asked what kind of relationships would I have with my friends and family? With the animals, planet, and earth?

Let's expand a little bit more on creating a relationship with someone. It's important to write a list of all of the things you would like the person to have as well as things that you would not like them to have. Being cute, but not bright, I wrote down a list of what I would like my play-mate to have, but not what I would not like him to have. So, as you can imagine, they had everything I desired AND everything I didn't desire.

So it's important to get clear on what you would like in a relationship because if you don't have clarity about what you truly wish to create as a relationship, you're probably not going to be pleased with the result! I'd like you to take a few minutes and write down a list of whatever you would like to create as a relationship.

Make two lists:

What would I LIKE to have in my relationship(s)?

What would I NOT LIKE to have in my relationship(s)?

What was cool about writing these lists is that I became aware of the energy of that person. Not, "I would like a man with blonde hair, blue eyes, and broad shoulders." I was able to start to receive the energy of what I desired instead of going just to looks, which is where I had functioned from in the past. We all know how well that turned out, don't we? Ha Ha!

Following the energy, I started playing with someone totally outside of this reality. We're having fun, and it's easy and light to be around him. This was totally outside of anything I could have planned or imagined. However, since I was aware of the energy and I was trusting myself, I chose to explore the relationship further. In the past I would have written off this relationship by going to my mind and thinking it through and going to the conclusion that it was never going to work.

By being able to perceive the energy of the partner or relationship I would like in my life, it was easy to follow the energy of someone that was going to be nurturing, honoring, fun to be around, and grateful for me. This was very different from the choices I had made in the past by just going on looks, job, money, etc. alone.

I did the same for work, finances, travel, etc. I got the way it would feel to have all of those things showing up. How I would feel on a daily basis if I could have it? Put that in there too.

Once you have an awareness of what you would like your life to be, put it in a ball out in front of you. This "energy ball" you created based on getting how it would "feel" to have your life show up the way you desire it is not actually based on just feelings. It's based on an awareness of the energy that would be there if you actually had what you are asking for.

Step 2

Once you have the energy ball in front of you, pull energy into it from all over the universe. Keep pulling, more, more, more, and even more. Pull from all over the universe!

What should be happening is your heart opening up as you pull more energy into these things you actually desire. When this occurs, be with the energy for a moment. Then, let little trickles go out to everyone and everything that's going to help make that a reality for you from all over the universe that you don't even know yet.

Step 3

This step is about following the energy. So go for that "feeling" because you'll be going for the energy of the living you'd like to create. And when somebody or something shows up, acknowledge that you are getting what you asked for. That's very important.

It is also important to stay in the question and not come to a conclusion when something or someone shows up that matches the energy. Continue to ask questions.

It's interesting that the elements of what I've desired to have in my life have changed over time as I've realized that what I thought I desired has turned out to not be what I actually desired. I wouldn't have really known this until I had a chance to experience it and then I could be clear that what I desired was something different. In the previous chapter, I started to realize how much I was choosing in my life for someone or something else. Again, as I began to choose more, I had more and more awareness of what I truly desired my life to be.

~ CHAPTER XXIV ~

NURTURE YOURSELF

*W*ow... I kept myself so busy like a "do-do bird" that I realized I had stopped nurturing myself and my body.

I started to look at what would be nurturing to me and my body. I started to ask questions such as, "What does my body require today and what could I do to nurture and care for myself and my body? What type of movement would my body enjoy? What would it take to be kind to me today?"

There was one question in particular that I heard that really rocked my world: "In what way could I treat myself like I should have been treated growing up?" Again, "In what way could I treat myself like I should have been treated growing up?" For me, that question shook me to my core as I realized that I was treating myself like I had been treated growing up – with very little care or gratitude.

When I asked this question, I started to be aware of how little I was actually honoring and caring for my body. How many times had I worked too hard and for too long, forced my body to stay up, drank and fed it too little or too much, or just plain totally disregarded it sexually? Countless times!

So, ask your body what would nurture it...what would make your body happy?

One really cool thing to do before getting up in the morning is to gently cup the sides of your cheeks and tell your body that you love it and that you are very grateful for it. Take a moment and try this. What energy comes up when you say that? How does your body feel? Is there more space and ease in your body?

You might start with apologizing to your body for not listening to it for all these years. Would you like to destroy and uncreate everything that doesn't allow you to perceive what would be honoring and nurturing to your body?

Do you know muscle testing? If so, use whatever technique you're familiar with. If not, this is the method I use when I ask my body what it desires. I stand with my heels together and ask my body a question. If it goes forward it's a yes and if it goes backward it's a no. If it goes side to side, it's a maybe or a sign I need to ask another question. There is not a right or a wrong way to do this. Ask your body to show you what a "yes" is and what a "no" is. Play with this and find out how your body communicates.

So take a moment and play with muscle testing and ask your body, what would nurture it? Write down three ways you can nurture your body:

1. _____

2. _____

3. _____

My body loves long, warm bubble baths with my favorite lavender mineral salts. I light scented candles and create a beautiful, relaxing space to totally unwind. I turn off all of the lights, turn off my cell phone ringer, and dedicate this time to nurturing myself. Afterward, my body loves warm coconut oil or body butter spread over my body. I especially like to massage my feet with my favorite lotion. Sometimes I have fun shaking talcum powder over my toes.

Have fun! Play! Ask your body what it requires to make it feel yummy and nurtured. Dance around like when you were a kid. My body also loves getting pedicures with an extra long massage. Especially deluxe pedicures with special salt scrubs.

I also find it very nurturing to go on quiet walks in the woods or in nature. I love to sit and take a few deep breaths and connect with the earth. Sitting quietly, listening, and becoming aware of the beauty around me is quite inspiring.

My body also loves energy work, especially the Bars which I explain in the glossary section. This process helps eliminate stress from the body and has many other incredible benefits.

Perhaps, begin with just a few hours a week to nurture yourself. Or, start with a few minutes in the morning cupping your cheeks. See if you perceive any difference and what works for you. Eventually, you may desire to nurture yourself one day/week or more if possible. Again, trust that you know what works for you.

When I started valuing myself to take the time to nurture me and my body, it totally changed how I treated myself. I began to be more gentle and grateful in everything that I did. I began to realize the areas in my life where I was basically abusing my body by forcing it to do things when it required rest. Enough was enough!

As I began to be grateful for me, there was a softness of energy that surrounded me. It's interesting, I even started to sit differently! For instance, I noticed that I was just shoving my body into a chair to sit down. Now when I sit down I gently and lovingly lower my body into the chair, treating my body like it is beautiful, delicate, and special. My body responds with gratitude as it enjoys being treated in such a special and caring way.

~ Chapter XXV ~

Stepping Into Joy and Ease

*I*f you were living your life today, what would you choose right away?

Begin to write down what it is that you would choose as your life today – right away! Look at what you would like. Not what your friends and family expect, not what your partner expects, not what your work expects, etc. And, would you please destroy and uncreate whatever doesn't allow you to have total clarity and ease with all of this?

What if you weren't willing to hold yourself back for anyone? What if you weren't willing to give up you for someone else? What if you began to see yourself as the gift you truly be? Start to actually look at what would work for you and what you would like.

This takes a lot of courage to really look at this. You get YOU in a way you never had before. It may seem a bit strange, but keep on keeping on! Trust YOU.

Look at what you would like, not how you have to fulfill someone else's needs. You have a choice. Someone else's needs are not more important than yours. Again, you have a choice. Trust YOU.

Every day, you may desire to ask, "If I was living my life today, what would I choose right away?"

Linda Wasil

Trust you. So, again, I'd like you to take a moment and find a quiet, private space. Take a few slow, deep breaths from the top of your head down to the tips of your little toes. Now, take another deep breath and start to expand out to the size of the room you're in. Now continue to expand out to the entire structure that you're in including the earth, the city block, your town, your state, your country, and to the galaxies. Continue to expand out. There's not a wrong or a right way to do this exercise. Just trust that when you ask, you're already becoming the space that you've asked for.

From this space, ask yourself, "If I was living my life today, what would I choose right away?"Again, ask yourself, "If I was living my life today, what would I choose right away?" Do you feel more like yourself after you ask this question? Do you have more space and ease?

Take a few moments in the space below to write down what awarenesses you have with this. Have fun with it! Play!

Perhaps reflecting on what you enjoyed doing as a child may give you clarity with this. Drawing, singing, skipping, playing, exploring, giggling, walking along the beach, building sand castles, playing on the swings, etc.

What is it that makes you laugh? What is it that brings you joy and makes your heart sing? This may be something that you could include on the list if it feels light to you. Trust what you know.

What if your life could actually be an adventure? What if it weren't about, "I've got to wake up again today and I've got to do this and I've got to do that?" What if you came out of obligation and into the adventure you could have as your life?

What if every morning you woke up and asked, "Who am I today and what grand and glorious adventures will I have?" Would that be a different way of waking up? I know for me it is. Just asking that question generates a different energy. I begin to access energies of adventure, possibility, and magic! So why not ask this question in the morning or at various times during the day?

What if you truly being you changed the world? Does that feel light to you? You know, there's no one quite like you in the whole wide world. What if by being you, you changed the world? What else is possible?

Linda Wasil

Thank you so much for reading my book. I'm so grateful for you! To finish, I'd like to repeat the quote in the beginning of the book:

"Our deepest fear is not that we are inadequate.

Our deepest fear is that we are powerful beyond measure.

It is our light not our darkness that frightens us."

~Marianne Williamson

With gratitude for the incredible YOU!

- Linda

PART III

Special Acknowledgment

I'd like to acknowledge the huge contribution that Dr. Dain Heer's book, *Being You, Changing The World*, has been to this project. I'm ever so grateful and how did I get so lucky to have so many amazing people like Dain and Gary willing to contribute to me on this project? It's been difficult at times (many, many times), I've shed many tears, and I'm so much stronger for it! What else is possible?! I've had to acknowledge the courage and strength that it's taken to write this book! Wow, I'm not a victim?! Is this turning into an acknowledgment of me? NO!! Say it isn't so?!

I highly, highly recommend Dain's book if you would like to learn additional tools and questions that you can use to create additional possibilities for your life and living. So, please ask, would his book be a contribution to my life and living? And… continue to trust that you know what works for you! You rock! Just trust that you know! Not me… not anyone else! You! Imagine that?

For more information on Dain's book visit:

www.beingyoubook.com

GLOSSARY

Explanation of the Access Clearing Statement

The clearing statement we use in Access Consciousness™ is: Right and wrong, good and bad, POD, POC, all nine, shorts, boys, and beyonds.

Right and Wrong, Good and Bad

Is shorthand for: What's good, perfect, and correct about this? What's wrong, mean, vicious, terrible, bad, and awful about this? What's right and wrong, good and bad?

POC

POC is the point of creation of the thoughts, feelings, and emotions immediately preceding whatever you decided.

POD

POD is the point of destruction immediately preceding whatever you decided. It's like pulling the bottom card out of a house of cards. The whole thing falls down.

All Nine

Stands for nine layers of crap that were taken out. You know that somewhere in those nine layers, there's got to be a pony because you couldn't put that much shit in one place without having a pony in there. It's shit that you're generating yourself, which is the bad part.

Shorts

Is the short version of: What's meaningful about this? What's meaningless about this? What's the punishment for this? What's the reward for this?

Boys

Stands for nucleated spheres. Have you ever been told you have to peel the layers of the onion to get to the core of an issue? Well, this is it – except it's not an onion. It's an energetic structure that looks like one. These are pre-verbal. Have you ever seen one of those kids' bubble pipes? Blow here and you create a mass of bubbles? As you pop one it fills back in. Basically these have to do with those areas of our life where we've tried to change something continuously with no effect. This is what keeps something repeating ad infinitum.

Beyonds

Are feelings or sensations you get that stop your heart, stop your breath, or stop your willingness to look at possibilities. It's like when your business is in the red and you get another final notice and you say, "argh!" You weren't expecting that right now.

Sometimes, instead of saying "use the clearing statement," we just say, "POD and POC it."

Be

In this book, the word *be* is sometimes used to refer to *you*, the infinite being you truly be, as opposed to a contrived point of view about who you think you are.

Explanation of The Bars

The Bars are a hands-on Access process that involves a light touch upon the head to contact points that correspond to different aspects of one's life. There are points for joy, sadness, body and sexuality, awareness, kindness, gratitude, peace and calm. There is even a money bar. These points are called bars because they run from one side of the head to the other.

Words have Energy

Words have energy to them. Every question we ask, every word we use, has an energy to it, and when we ask a question, that energy goes into action.

How often do you say, "I want"? In modern dictionaries, the word want means to desire, but in dictionaries published prior to 1946, there are twenty-six definitions for want which mean to lack. So, I encourage you to access a dictionary prior to 1946 and begin to look at the definitions of what you are saying and you may find that a word has a total different energy than what you think you are saying. For instance, if you would like more money in your life you might say, "I don't want more money" ten times and see how you feel. Do you feel lighter? You feel lighter because you are saying, "I don't lack of more money," which means you are now willing to have more money in your life.

Truth versus True

Truth and what is true are two different energies. Truth is a fixed point of view; it is an answer and usually a judgment. A truth is a solidity whereas true is a perception of what is in this moment. It can change. That which is a truth becomes a fixed point of view, which stops the energy and leaves you stuck in it. Have you ever had someone tell you "their truth" about you? I have and it felt really heavy!

ACCESS CONSCIOUSNESS™ RESOURCES

Some ways to connect and find out about
Access Consciousness™ online:

www.AccessConsciousness.com

www.DrDainHeer.com

www.GaryMDouglas.com

www.BeingYouBook.com

www.ConsciousHorseConsciousRider.com

www.AccessJoyofBusiness.com

www.onlinerecoverycenter.com

www.SuzyGodsey.com

www.FacilitatingtheEarth.com

http://transformationallivinginconsciousness.com

ABOUT THE AUTHOR

Linda Wasil is a consultant, transformational coach, author, speaker, and facilitator of Access Consciousness™. For more than thirteen years she has facilitated clients all over the world in living their dream of a happier, more fulfilling life through individual sessions, workshops, and presentations.

She is expanding her energy work to include animals, big and small, and is a Certified Facilitator of Conscious Horse, Conscious Rider™. She shares her life with her dog Coco and horses.

To learn more about Linda and her presentations and workshops, visit:

www.LindaWasil.com or

www.BeyondtheStigmaofAbuse.com.

What would the world be like if each of us recognized the gift and contribution we truly are?

How does it get even better than this?

What else is possible?

Coco the "Wonderdog"

Found running wild in the rainforest in Costa Rica. Here's a girl that knows what she desires and goes for it! I've learned so much from her. She's been an amazing friend and has brought so much joy into my life. How did I get so lucky?

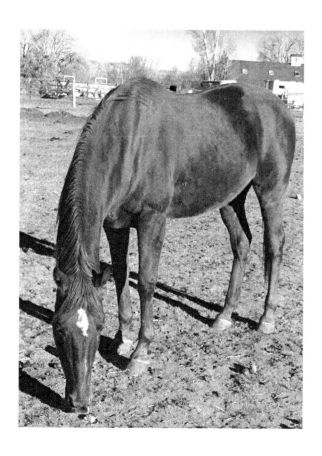

Copper

Her beautiful coat radiates in the sun. She, like Coco, knows what she desires and keeps me on my toes. She's teaching me how to ride and is a great facilitator; gently nudging me to be ever more aware, joyful, and the leader I truly be. What else is possible?

OTHER BOOKS BY LINDA WASIL

Speaking Your Truth, Volume II

Courageous Stories from Inspiring Women

By Lisa Shultz & Andrea Constantine

Linda is a contributing author of this Amazon bestseller. This is an inspirational compilation of stories by women which inspires a different possibility for living.

Financial Fit Females

By Sharlene Douthit

Linda is a contributing author of this soon-to-be-released book which inspires women to different possibilities with abundance, wealth, and finance.

Look for Linda's children's book to be released in late 2012.

CPSIA information can be obtained at www.ICGtesting.com
Printed in the USA
BVOW020140190912

300724BV00005B/1/P

9 781938 487026